'KNOW THE GAME' SERIES

KAYAK CANOEING

Published in collaboration with
THE BRITISH CANOE UNION

E P PUBLISHING Ltd.

CONTENTS

FOREWORD

The canoe is the oldest form of true boat, having been used from time immemorial in all parts of the world, for transport, hunting and travel. Canoe designs have varied widely depending on the use to which the canoe was to be put and the materials available to the builder. Thus we have, for example, the 'dug-out' of the tropical forests, the 'birchbark' of the North American Indian, the sealskin covered 'kayak' of the Eskimo and the long 'war canoe' of the South Seas, each a specialised instrument. Although the canoe has been used from ancient times it has not suffered obsolescence, and it can still be found in use in many parts of the world, surviving because it does its job so efficiently.

The modern sport and recreation of CANOEING began rather more than a century ago when a certain John MacGregor had a kayak built of oak and cedar, named it the 'Rob Roy' and in it travelled widely on the rivers, lakes and seas of Europe and the Near East. His exploits were reported in the national newspapers, and on his return he lectured and wrote books on his travels. All this captured the imagination of the sportsmen of the day and they urged MacGregor to form a club to foster and promote this novel adventurous activity. 'The Canoe Club' was duly formed in 1866, to become a few years later, 'The Royal Canoe Club' with Edward, Prince of Wales, as its Commodore, and this club still exists by the River Thames below Kingston, and is one of the leading clubs in Britain. And so the sport of CANOEING was inaugurated and since that time has spread over the whole world with adherents numbered in millions.

This is the multi-sided activity which Oliver Cock, Director of Coaching in the British Canoe Union, is introducing in this booklet. I hope his enthusiasm will prove infectious and that many of those who read it will act upon his advice and try their hand at a most satisfying recreation. Canoeing caters for all ages and temperaments, for those who enjoy good company and those who prefer solitude, for all who find enjoyment on the water whether it takes the form of a meandering stream, mountain torrent or the open sea.

John Dudderidge

President,
British Canoe Union.

INTRODUCTION

This little book is intended to start you on your way in using a Kayak canoe. Some mention is made of the Canadian canoe—or North American Indian canoe as it should more rightly be called—but, although there is a similarity in the handling of the two types of canoe, it really needs another book of this sort to start you off in the Canadian.

This book will therefore set you going in your Kayak, and it will briefly give you ideas on what you can do when you have learnt how to handle it. It is possible to get into a Kayak and paddle off straight away. But such a way is fraught with hidden dangers—hidden because of your ignorance of them. Learn about them; get someone to tell you about them; and the dangers disappear because you now know about them. Indeed, some of the things that look like being dangerous turn out to be quite safe, and in the same way some of the places that look perfectly safe, turn out to be places which you must avoid.

Even the handling of the canoe is not as easy as all that, if you want to be good at it. It will need a lot of practice on your part before you become proficient; but when you are really good, all sorts of adventures are opened up to you, because this apparently funny, frail little vessel can take you places where no other vessel can go.

On the other hand, if you have a mind for it, you can just potter. It is just as much fun in its way.

TYPES OF CANOE

A K.1 Racing Kayak

One thing you must do first is to try all sorts of canoes, to see which one you prefer. The next few pages will show you some of these various sorts, and later we will give you some ideas as to some of the places in which you might find them.

This canoe is a single-seat racing Kayak—hence the title 'K.1'. There are also 'K.2's' and K.4's'. You can use them for Sprint racing or for Long Distance racing. You can even use them for light-weight touring; that is to say that you are not carrying very much luggage with you. On the whole they prefer calm water to rough.

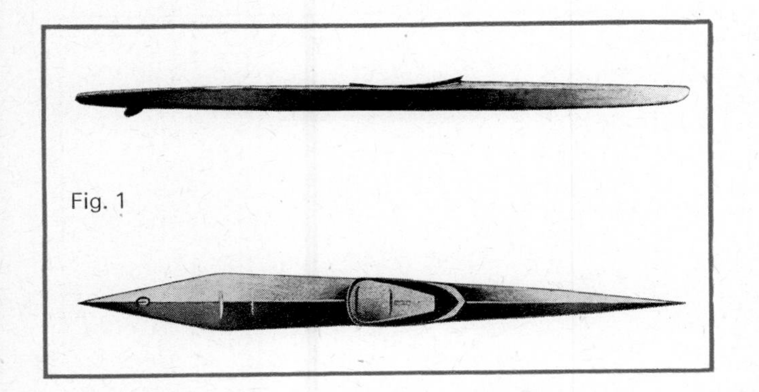

Fig. 1

A K.1 Slalom Kayak

A racing Kayak likes to go in straight lines, because that is the way one races.

On the other hand a slalom canoe has to be very manoeuvrable. It also has to be able to ride very rough rapids. Water like this is called 'white water' because the foam makes it appear white.

If it is difficult to make a racing Kayak turn, so it is difficult to make a slalom Kayak go straight. Like the racing canoe, you cannot pack much luggage in it—which is just as well because you do not want to have to handle any more weight than you must when you are on those rapids.

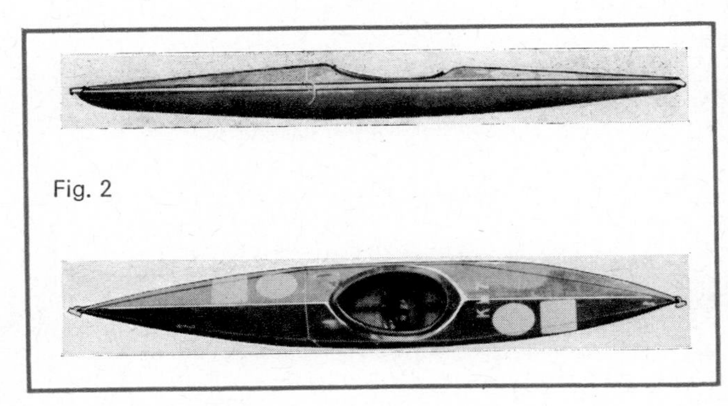

Fig. 2

A K.1 Touring Kayak

If the last two Kayaks were extreme in their own ways, one wanting to go straight and the other wanting only to go round in circles, so some sort of compromise has to be reached if you want to do both. The trouble is that a canoe that does both does neither as efficiently as the others! However, if you just want to go on trips down rivers, there is ample room in this Kayak for all the luggage that you might like to carry—always remembering that the more you carry the more you have to push along.

You will also see that the cockpit is bigger, giving you more room to move about—but do remember that if you do move you still have to balance the thing.

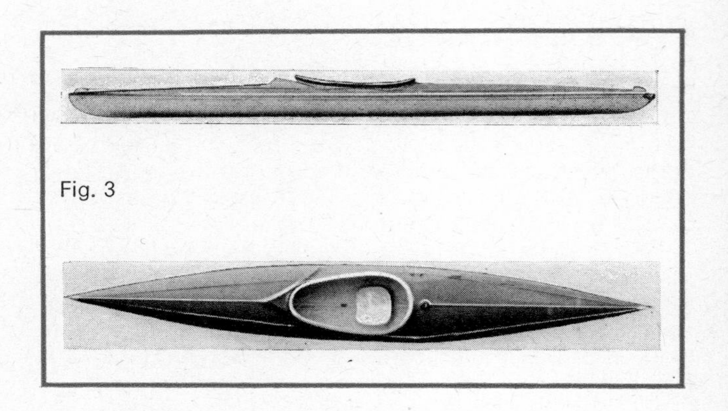

Fig. 3

A BAT Canoe

These canoes were originally designed for use in swimming baths, to teach people canoeing there. They took an ordinary canoe, chopped off the ends and rounded off the middle bit and there you were.

Then somebody thought of playing a form of water polo in canoes, and these canoes—properly called Baths Advanced Trainers—were found to be ideal.

Although they are 'fun' canoes, they are not a lot of use for canoeing on rivers or the sea. They are too much like hard work to push along.

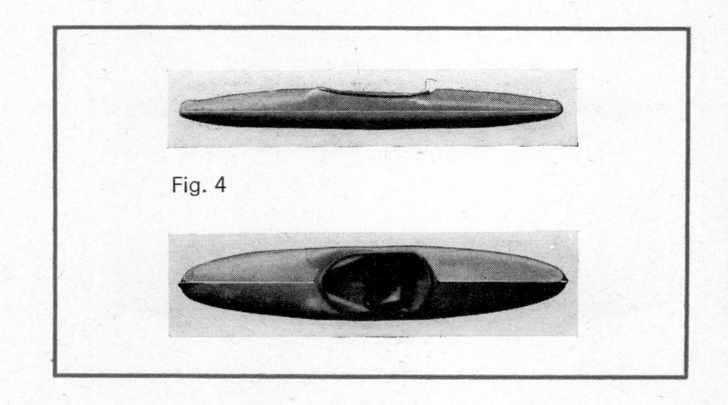

Fig. 4

A Canadian Touring Canoe

This is the sort of canoe in which you would expect to see Red Indians paddling, but it is also the great canoe with which people travel through the backwoods of Canada, carrying all their gear with them. It is a wonderful canoe to tour in, making part of your bivouac cover for the night as well.

Unlike the Kayak, it is usually propelled with a paddle that has a blade at one end only. This one is a three-seater, but they can be single, double, or almost anything else you like. Since it is a 'commercial' boat, as opposed to a competition boat, you can move it along how you like, according to the circumstances. You can use a double-bladed paddle, or a punt pole, or even an engine if you must, but it is quieter and cleaner without that sort of thing.

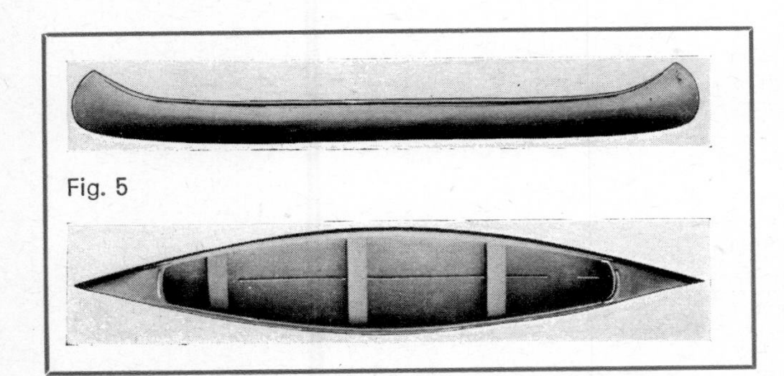

Fig. 5

A C.1 Slalom Canoe

The touring Canadian sometimes has to shoot rapids. Being an open boat, it cannot meet very heavy water. Modern building materials such as glass re-inforced plastic have allowed us to deck it in and produce this Canadian canoe for slaloms. As this is a competition canoe, the single-bladed paddle is always used, and you paddle on one side only. This type of canoe can also be a two-seater or a double (C.2), when one person paddles on one side and the other on the other. On rapids they are probably the most versatile of any canoe, and they can go into places where no other craft can get.

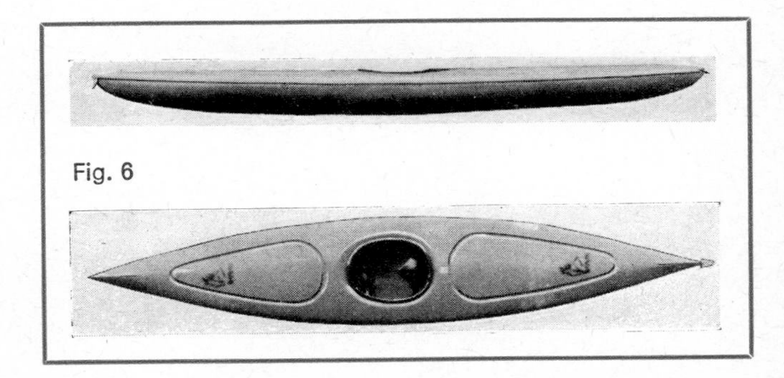

Fig. 6

A Sea Touring Canoe

Back among the Kayaks again, this one is longer and slimmer than most of the others. This enables it to cut smoothly through the water and remain unaffected by the waves. Since it is also narrow-beamed and you sit very low in it, the waves do not make it roll. It is rather like riding a bicycle over rough ground, as opposed to a tricycle. The bicycle only feels the bumps along its length, but the tricycle feels them sideways as well.

This canoe is not very manoeuvrable, preferring rather to go in straight lines. However, there is a lot of room at sea and so the need to turn is less important.

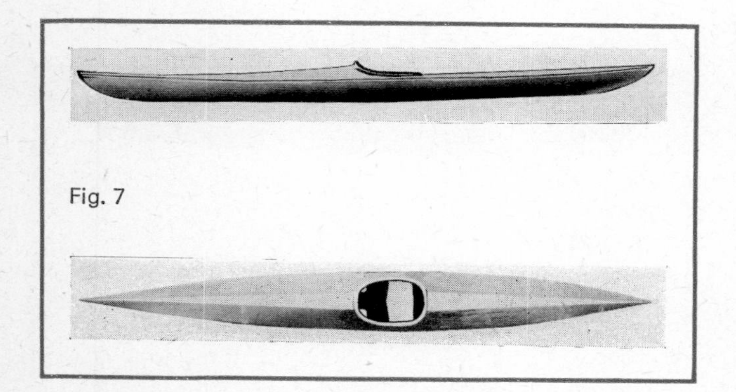

Fig. 7

A Rescue Canoe

Here is a canoe that has been developed specially for the Corps of Canoe Life Guards. These life guards will patrol anywhere where people may have swimming accidents. They are also likely to patrol at sailing regattas, where a sudden squall may put a number of sailing dinghies into difficulties at one time. They go with long-distance swimmers as their escort boats. They go with free-diving swimmers. They have been out with lifeboats, and have been able to get closer to vessels in distress than the lifeboat can manage because of its deep draft.

The Corps offers a service which, in collaboration with other services, provides a life-saving protection as complete as anything possible.

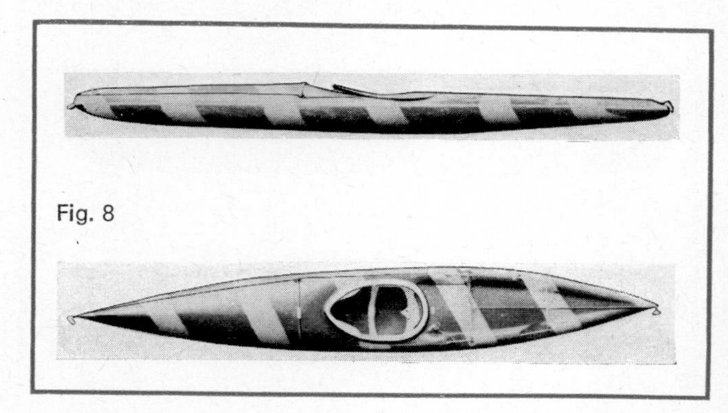

Fig. 8

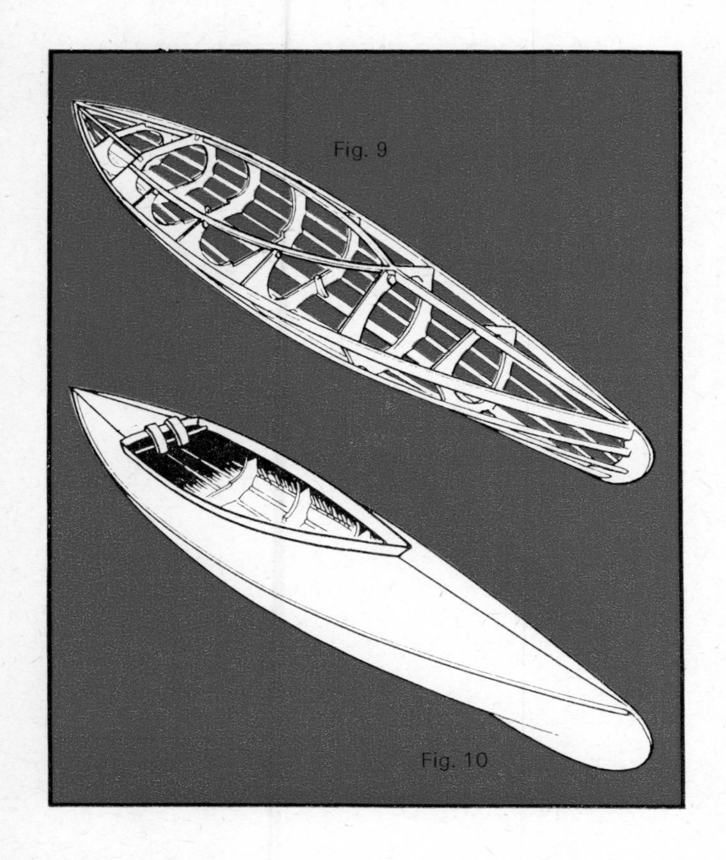

METHODS OF CONSTRUCTION

Canvas Covered Canoes

There are many ways of making a canoe. In this little book we can only give you a brief look at three methods, leaving you to make your own choice and learn more about it.

These two pictures show you a method which is dying out now; this is to build a frame of wood and then to stretch a skin of canvas over it. This is a very old method of making a boat, needing not a great deal of skill to make it; but the finished vessel is rather frail and needs a very great deal of attention and maintenance afterwards.

There should be a seat and a footrest. These two pieces of comfort should always be in every canoe, and the footrest should be so made that you cannot possibly get your foot past it; otherwise you may not be able to get it back again, when you want to get out.

Fig. 9 The Frame. Fig. 10 The covered canoe.

Fig. 11

A Folding Canoe

A variation of the rigid skin-frame canoe is the folding canoe. Here the framework within the skin can be 'broken' in the cockpit area and withdrawn from the skin. Then the framework is broken down even further and the whole lot is packed away into bags for easy transport to other places.

This is its virtue. In its bags you can take it by train or how you will to where you want to start your trip. You build it in half an hour, set off, finish your trip, pack up and go home.

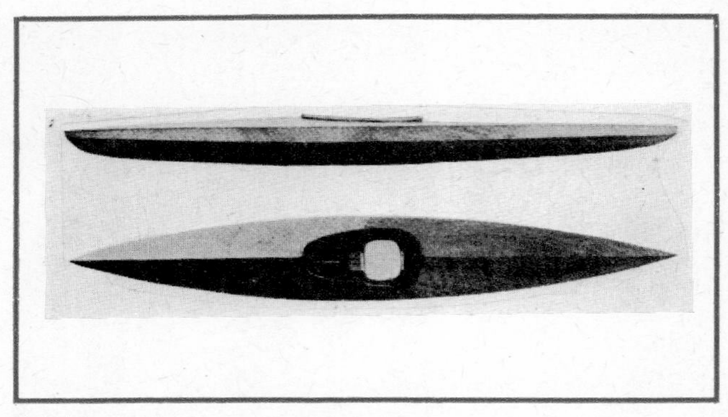

Fig. 12

The 'Kayel' Construction

This is a way of making a 'hard chine' canoe out of sheets of plywood. It was invented by a Mr. Ken Littledyke out of whose initials the word 'Kayel' derives.

Boats made of wood are always beautiful, especially as they get older, if they are properly maintained. There is always this problem of maintenance, though this is less so with Kayel canoes than with either of the skin-over-frame constructions. The method of construction is supremely easy and very fast, so it is well worth thinking of if you are going to build your own canoe. We give a few details of the method on the next page.

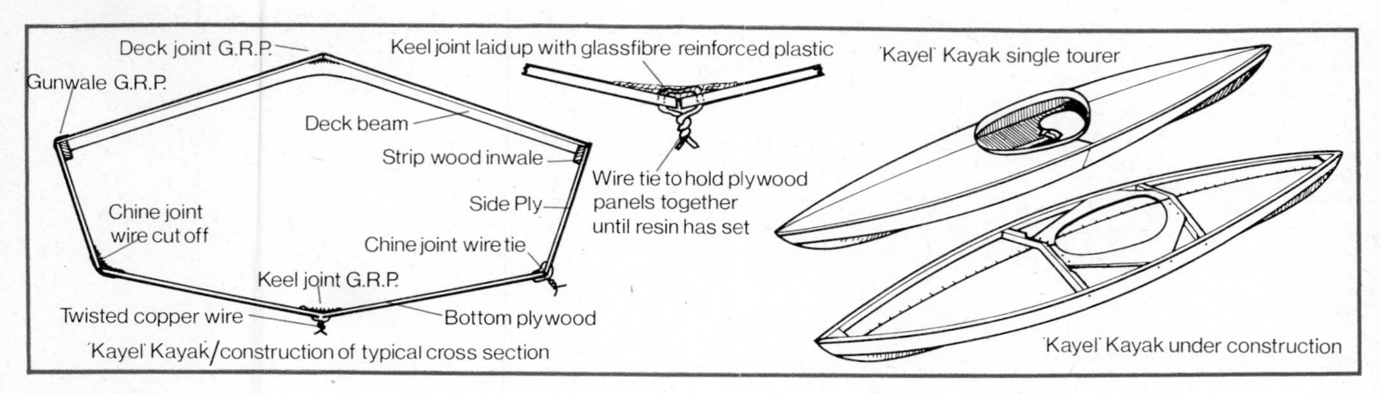

Figs. 13 and 14

The Method

A Kayel Kayak is made for the most part of sheets of marine plywood cut to shape and sewn together, either by little bits of copper wire as shown, or by nylon thread, and then the joint is covered over on the inside by glass tape 1" wide to make it watertight. When the resin holding the tape has gone hard any protruding twists of wire can be cut off and smoothed down to leave a smooth finish.

This is done on the keel line, the chine and the deck line, but the deck and the hull have to be put together in the more 'traditional' way by a strip of wood laid inside the gunwale on the hull, and the deck fastened to that.

An extra thickness of plywood is laid around and underneath the cockpit opening, and the cockpit coaming is built up on that. Seat and footrest are added and remarkably quickly you have completed your canoe. All that remains, now, is to give it its coats of varnish.

An advantage of this system of construction is that few special tools or space are required. Except for the sticking down of the glass tape and other joints, and the varnishing, none of the work is dirty. We have known people who have made this sort of canoe in their bedrooms.

The G.R.P. Canoe

There remains space for only one more method of construction. This is that of glass-reinforced plastic (G.R.P.) or glassfibre as it is popularly known. Again, the method is simple, but it is complicated by the necessity of having a mould into which you shape your canoe. One person can make the canoe by himself, but it is better, simpler and faster to have a team. There is a certain amount of chemistry involved which can go badly wrong if you do not know how to do it. It can waste a great deal of your money or, worse still, you can have an explosion.

Nevertheless the method is very simple once you have learnt how. Therefore, please either find somebody who knows all about it to help you or, if you cannot do that (and it will surprise us if you cannot, because more and more people know about it nowadays), then buy books about it, study them carefully and learn that way—but it is much harder than getting someone to help!

The canoes that you will make are perhaps not as elegant as the wooden ones, but they are not unattractive. They come in all shapes and sizes so you are sure to find one that suits you.

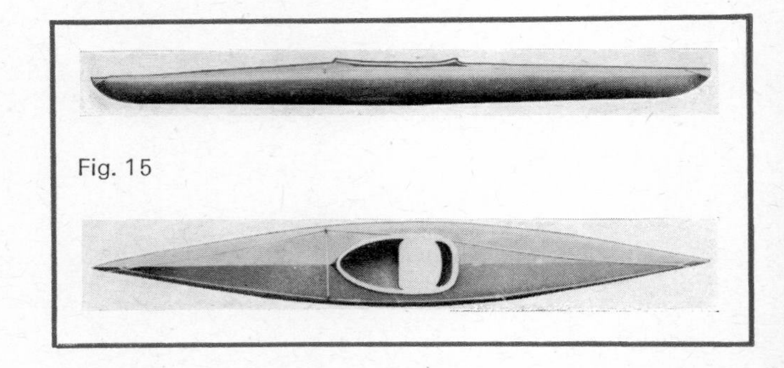

Fig. 15

Fig. 16

Fig. 17

EQUIPMENT

Fully equipped summer canoeist

There is not a very great deal of equipment that you need with your canoe. The person above is properly dressed and equipped to go on a summer cruise. Let us see what he should have.

A Spray Cover

Firstly we show a spray cover. This might be described as a necessary luxury, because it makes life so much more comfortable. The tube part fits closely round your waist like a tummy-band. The other part is usually sprung over the cockpit coaming by an elastic so that you wear it all the time, and it springs on and off your canoe.

Notice the special release strap at the front so that you can pull it easily when you want to. All spray covers should have something by which you can pull them off in this way.

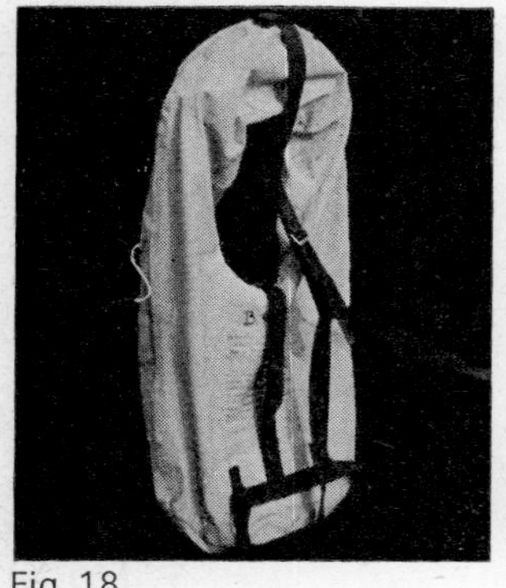

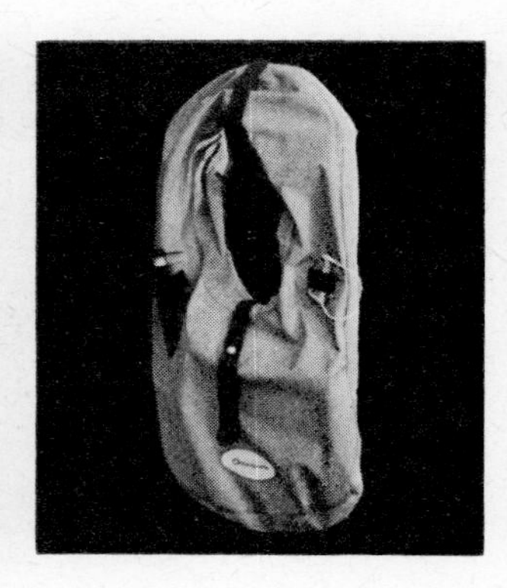

Fig. 18

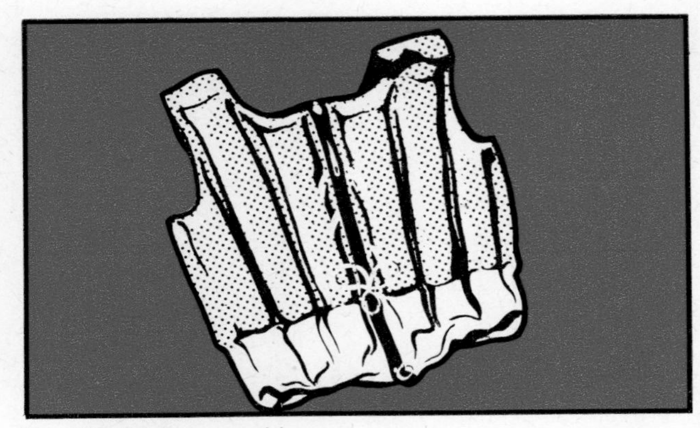

Fig. 19 A buoyancy aid

A Life Saving Jacket

An essential in your equipment is a life jacket. If you really want it to look after you when you are in trouble, then it should have on it a British Standard Kite mark and the number B.S. 3595.

There are many types. The one we recommend is a 'two-stage' jacket, with an inherent stage of $13\frac{1}{2}$lbs to make sure you float, and an inflatable stage to over 35lbs of buoyancy which will put you comfortably on your back while you wait for help to arrive.

A Buoyancy Aid

This type of jacket does not have the two stages of the life-saving jacket. Instead it has only one, similar to the lower stage of the British Standard one. Thus it will help you float, and it has the advantage of keeping you warm in cold weather; but it will do nothing to try to save your life should you be in real trouble.

We might suggest that you could wear this type of jacket on little rivers, where you know you are going to be able to get to dry land very quickly, but that, where you are not going to be able to get to dry land quickly you ought to have the one with the Kite mark on it.

A Buoyancy Bag

Having got your own buoyancy, you have now got to have some buoyancy for your canoe, to make sure that it stays afloat. Very often the makers fix in blocks of polystyrene at each end, but anything that is really buoyant will do. We have illustrated an air bag which is specially shaped to be fixed up at either end of the canoe (there ought to be two, one for each end). The minimum sensible amount of buoyancy at each end is 30lbs, making a total of 60lbs, but you can put in as much more as you like.

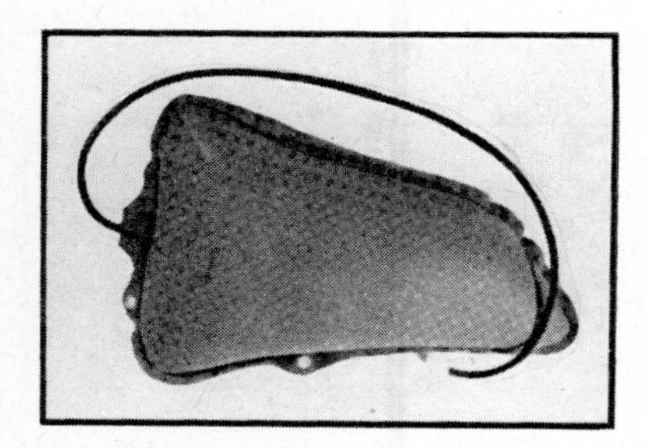

Fig. 20

Paddles

Lastly of the bigger stuff, the tool with which you're going to move your Kayak about—your paddle.

The top picture (Fig. 21a) shows a good class, spoon-bladed paddle for the Kayak. Notice that the two blades are at right-angles to each other. We will

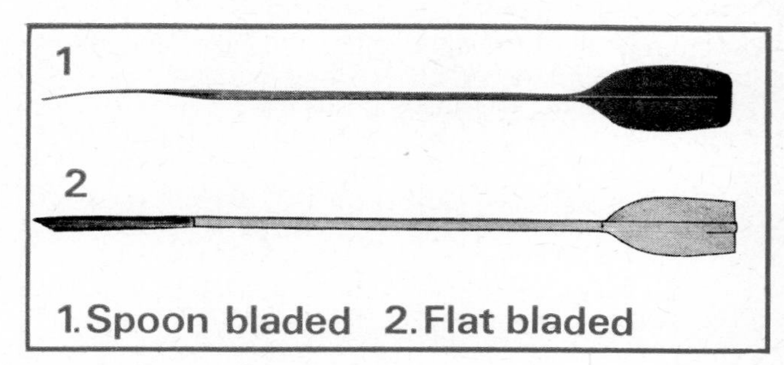

Fig. 21a and b

Fig. 22a and b

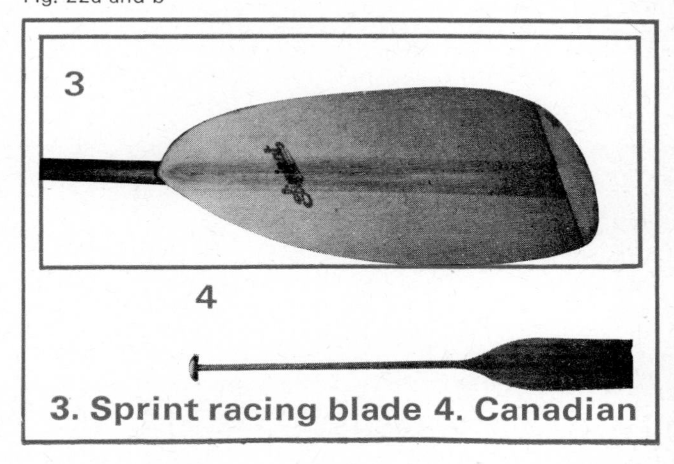

describe how you deal with this later on. This paddle, however, is rather expensive, and you may prefer to have something cheaper to start with. So the next picture (Fig. 21b) shows you a flat-bladed paddle which is made with plywood blades, and an aluminium loom (that is the middle round part) which is covered with plastic to make it more comfortable.

Of the two in the lower illustrations, the upper one (Fig. 22a) is especially for sprint racing people. The blades are kidney-shaped, or asymmetrical, so that the pressure of the water on the blade is always exactly up the middle of the loom.

Right at the bottom (Fig. 22b) is a picture of one of many sorts of paddle to be used with the Canadian canoe. Unlike the Kayak paddles, it has only one blade, which is always symmetrical, and there is a hand-grip at the other end.

Finally we come to the bits and pieces. The illustration shows a canoe with a painter fastened at the bow and the stern. There are many ways of arranging your painter, most of them good, but a few not good. To judge whether your way is good or bad, answer these two questions: (i) Does it ever get in your way as you try to get in or out? Answer Yes (BAD) No (GOOD); (ii) Can you free it easily so that you can use it to tie your canoe to the bank? Answer Yes (GOOD) No (BAD).

One of the little pictures shows a toggle secured to the bow of the canoe. There should be another at the stern, and the length of the toggle should be 3 to 4 inches so that you can hold onto it firmly. You could possibly have just a loop instead, but this must be made of rope of minimum diameter 3 mm. and big enough, again to get hold of it properly; otherwise you stand to lose a finger if you get twisted up in it. The one remaining picture shows a crash helmet specially made for canoeists so that the water pours out of it should they find themselves upside down at some time. This piece of equipment is made specially for the white water canoeist.

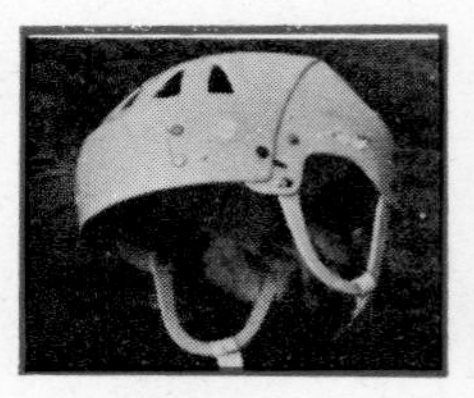

A crash helmet

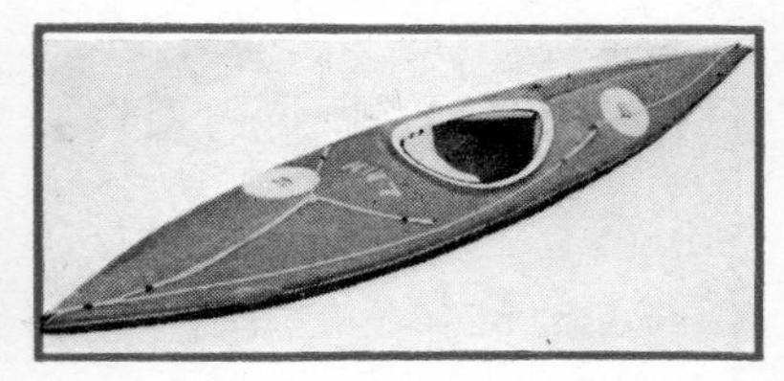

Canoe with painter

A Bow Toggle

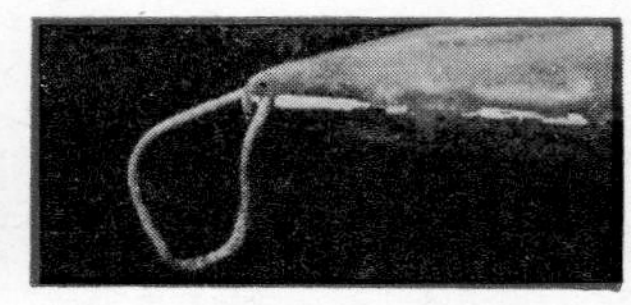

A Bow Loop

Fig. 24 Summer Canoeist

Winter Canoeist

CLOTHING

It makes a difference to what you wear, whether you are going to canoe in the summer or the winter. In warm weather ordinary football gear (less the boots!) may be alright; but you will die of cold if that is all you wear in the winter.

So, taking summer weather first, we will say that football clothing is about right, as you can always put on an extra sweater, or an anorak or smock if you feel cold, or better still, you can start with too much on and take things off as you get hot. But you must have something on your feet, and we suggest that gym shoes are the right sort of things as you can swim in them quite easily and they protect your feet against the broken bottles and sharp stones and things that always seem to be lying about nowadays.

But in the winter you have got to protect yourself against the cold. This is where the wet-suit or the dry-suit comes into its own. Whether it be a full suit as illustrated, or a 'shortie' or how you like is up to you. You can make it yourself or you can buy one ready made; but it is essential that you protect yourself against the cold, otherwise you are possibly going to be very seriously ill.

Fig. 25 Winter and Summer canoeists

Fig. 26 The Anorak and the Smock

The Anorak and Smock

If you can dress 'how you like' up to a point, the anorak and the smock are two of the most useful garments that you can wear. They are comfortable. They are wind-proof. They can be water-proof and are at least shower-proof.

The difference between the two garments is that the anorak is waisted and therefore has a short skirt, whereas the smock has no skirt. The tightening cord being right round the base. The skirt of the anorak can be a bit much as you sit in your canoe with your spray cover on. Therefore the smock is perhaps the better garment.

Both of them should have hoods, as it is very important to keep the back of your head warm in adverse weather. You could wear a scarf, but that gets wet when it rains so we recommend a hooded anorak as being better.

This garment even pays when you wear it over the top of a wet suit, as it acts as a wind-cheater in cold conditions, when the wet suit alone is not enough to keep you warm. Please remember, though, that it is going to get wet and therefore you should have one that dries fairly easily. The heavy cloth, 'army' type is too heavy when it is soaking wet.

Canoe Clubs and Organisations

In our introduction right at the beginning we suggested that you should find someone to help you learn how to canoe. There are many establishments, all over the country, which are very willing to help you like this. One of the best methods is to approach the British Canoe Union, which is the governing body of the sport of canoeing, throughout the United Kingdom and represents us on the International Canoe Federations, the international governing body. They have a Coaching Scheme, covering the whole of the United Kingdom with Area Coaching Organisers and Local Coaching Organisers who are there for the very purpose of helping you. There are Competition Coaches, as well, so that whatever you want to do there is somebody waiting to help

The Sports Council also runs courses in canoeing, at almost any level. Bisham Abbey National Sports Centre near Marlow runs courses up to a moderate level, and Plas y Brenin National Mountain Centre runs courses up to a high level of skill.

The addresses of these organisations are given on pages 47 and 48. Write to them and they will do all they can to help you.

As well as these nearly every Education Authority in the country has a centre, and you might well need only to ask them to get on a course.

After this, there are many canoe clubs all over the country, and again the B.C.U. can help you. Ask them where your nearest suitable club is, and they will send you the name and address of the person to whom to write. It is worth joining a club.

Fig. 27 Teacher with rafted class

Fig. 28

Carrying a canoe on your shoulder

Obviously the first things that you have to learn are how to carry your canoe to the starting place, and then how to take it to the water's edge.

To carry the canoe some distance most comfortably you put it with the cockpit coaming resting on your shoulder, and your paddle in your other hand as you see in Fig. 28. You will find your canoe balancing very nicely in that position.

Carrying a canoe to the water

Having arrived, you take your canoe to the water's edge as shown in Fig. 29, by grasping it and your paddle in both hands, again by the cockpit until you are right by the water.

At the water put it carefully onto the water and keep hold of it, otherwise it will float away.

Getting in

To get in, keep your paddle close to you or lying across the canoe and the shore, put the hand that is nearest the water onto the prow of the cockpit and keep the other hand on the shore. Now for a brief balancing act! Put the foot nearest the water into the cockpit and as far forward as you dare. Bring the other foot in beside it, behind it or right down inside and SIT DOWN. And the quicker you do *that*, the better!

Fig. 29

Fig. 30 Getting in and out

Getting out is exactly the same thing done backwards. Draw the foot furthest from the land up under your seat (you can help by pulling it there with one hand). One hand goes to the land and holds on while the other grasps the prow of the cockpit. Pull yourself up and step ashore. Don't do the splits! It will only make your friends laugh and you wet!

Fig. 31

Sitting properly

Once in your canoe you should sit properly. Sit upright and have your feet resting properly on your footrest. You may, if you like, have places where you can grip your knees. This will certainly help you steady your canoe if it gets bumped about a bit on rough water. Your canoe needs to be balanced so you must not wriggle from side to side nor try to push yourself up by pushing down on the canoe on one side only. If you must adjust your position, put a hand on both sides of the canoe and lift yourself that way. This will keep the canoe balanced properly.

Paddling

We shall be going into the technique of paddling more thoroughly later on. For the moment let us just say that you remain in this same sitting position all the

Fig. 32

time. You hold the paddle balanced between your two hands, and as you pull one blade back through the water you push the other one forward through the air so that it is ready for the next stroke. Do not lean forward, nor lean back, nor swing from one side to the other. Just remain sitting upright, with your arms and your shoulders working the paddle.

Later on you will find you can lean over sideways in your Kayak, but even then it comes with you, as when taking a bicycle round a corner. All this will be disclosed when we come to technique.

DO's and DON'Ts for Canoeists

DON'T canoe if you cannot swim

DO provide buoyancy: always air bags in your boat, and a life jacket for yourself where a capsize would be dangerous—in the sea, heavy rapids, floods, and cold water.

DO ask about local conditions: tides, currents, rapids, and weather changes can all be dangerous.

DON'T go out alone without having told someone where you are going and how long you think you will be.

DON'T put more people in a canoe than it is designed to carry.

DON'T wear wellingtons. You cannot swim in heavy boots.

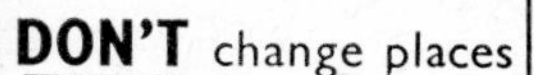

DON'T change places

DO keep clear of other craft.

DO keep away from weirs. They are dangerous.

DON'T right a capsized canoe. Hang on to it. It will float and you may not.

DON'T be put off by this list. It is all common sense really.

DO REMEMBER —better safe than sorry.

DO learn to canoe properly and take the B.C.U. Tests

For information apply to your Club Secretary, or to the BRITISH CANOE UNION 26, PARK CRESCENT, LONDON W1N 4DT.

Fig. 33

The Capsize Drill

Fig. 34

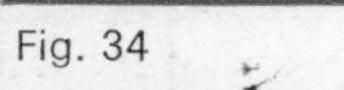

Fig. 35

Fig. 35a

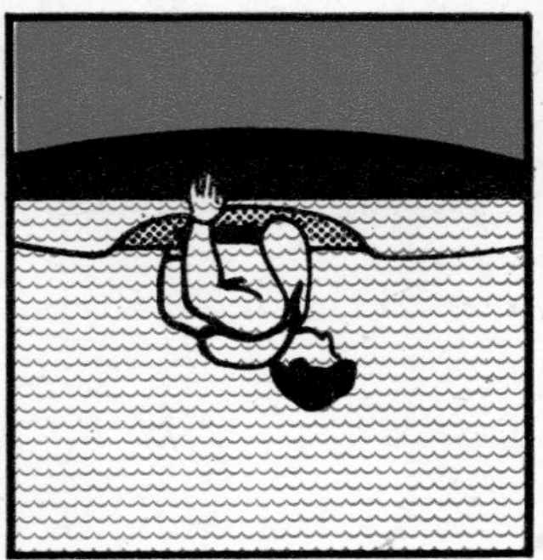

Fig. 36

Fig. 37

Fig. 38

Fig. 39

Fig. 34	Holding canoe before capsize.
Fig. 35	Capsized.
Fig. 35a	Capsized, taking spray cover off.
Fig. 36	Pushing out.
Fig. 37	Towing canoe ashore.
Fig .38	Emptying canoe (lifting up).
Fig. 39	Emptying canoe (pushing down).

SAFETY

If you have looked at the list of Dos and Don'ts on page 23 carefully enough you will have noticed that some emphasis is put on the fact that you are going to find yourself swimming. Now, swimming in itself is harmless enough, but it can be frightening if it is unexpected. Therefore, we earnestly advise you to practise capsizing your canoe, bringing it ashore and emptying it out so that you can go on again. We have already indicated that your clothing and equipment have got to be suitable for swimming in, so it is as well if you learn and practise, as much as you like. Actually, you will find to your amazement that it is great fun when you have got used to it. If you are a little scared now, that is because you have not practised. If you want to be a good and safe canoeist then this is the way to do it.

Firstly you must lean forward (Fig. 34) and remain that way even when you are upside down (Fig. 35).

Secondly pull the spray cover off by its release strap, if you have the cover on. (Fig. 35a).

Thirdly you take your hands to behind you on the canoe (Fig. 36) and push yourself out and downwards, still leaning forwards.

Fourthly, when you are clear of the cockpit, surface and go to the nearest end of your canoe, and tow it ashore (Fig. 37).

Once in shallow water or by the water's edge, lift your end up high to drain the water out (Fig. 38). Then turn it over and push it down again until what water remains is at your end (Fig. 39). Then pick it up and turn it over in one movement until you are again in your first position (Fig. 38). Go on doing this until all the water is drained out and you can get in again.

Practise this until you become really proficient at it.

CHOICE OF PADDLE

There is only one drill which you now ought to do before you set off. This is to choose your correct length of paddle and to learn how to use it.

The correct length for you yourself may be different after a time, but a very good starting point is to have the paddle vertical beside you, to raise your hand and just comfortably curl your fingers over the top of it. (Fig. 40a).

To find where you should put your hands on the loom, balance the paddle on top of your head and then grasp it with both hands so that your elbows make a right angle (Fig. 41). If you do find that this is a bit too wide apart, you may bring your hands in until you are just about in the 'arms bend' position; but do not go outside or inside these two limits.

The last bit, now, is to find out which hand will hold the loom firmly, and which will allow the loom to slide round in it. So pretend you are paddling and see if you can determine this. If you cannot do it now, it will come quite quickly when you start paddling for real.

Incidentally, the paddles with spoon or curved blades are 'handed'. The way to find out if the one you have is right for you, is to put the paddle vertically in front of you with the hollow of the lower blade towards your feet. Then the hollow of the blade above you should face towards your gripping hand. The man on the right in Fig. 40b is holding a right handed paddle.

Fig. 40a Length of paddle

Fig. 40b Handed Paddle

Fig 41

Fig. 42

Fig. 43

THE PADDLING STROKES

The Racing Stroke

Starting by putting the right blade into the water, the right arm and shoulder are fully extended, assisting this by a slight twist at the waist. The left elbow is raised and the left hand is about eye level. You are sitting upright, with a straight back. (Fig. 42.)

Now pull the right blade back, at the same time the left arm should push straight forward until, when the right elbow reaches your hip the left arm is fully extended and you have twisted your shoulders to the right. (Fig. 44.)

Fig. 44

When the right elbow is at your hip, the right blade is taken out of the water until your right hand is in the same position on its side of your face to where your left hand was at the beginning (Fig. 44).

Now drop the left blade into the water and continue paddling. Try to make this a smooth, continuous flow of movement, with a gentle twist of your body as you move rhythmically along. As you pull the right blade back, so your right foot should press on the footrest, similarly left blade, left foot.

It will take time for you to become really efficient at this; but it will be worth it, and make your paddling that much more easy.

Fig. 45

Paddling Backwards

If in paddling forwards you reached forwards to put the blade in the water, now you must reach backwards, looking over your shoulder as you do so. Notice that you use the back of the blade as you push yourself backwards, and be careful that it strikes the water flat as it goes; otherwise you will be in trouble.

Again, the blade is taken from the water as your elbow passes your hip, and there is plenty of twist at your waist, this being assisted as you look over each shoulder in turn.

Having learnt to paddle forwards and backwards, you must now learn to manoeuvre your canoe.

Fig. 46

Fig. 47 Bow Sweep

Fig. 48 Stern Sweep

The Sweep

We can pair these manoeuvring strokes, and by good luck the first pair have a single name—The Sweep. The first half of it is known as the Bow Sweep, and the second half as the Stern Sweep. The object of the stroke, or its parts, is to turn the canoe.

To do the Bow Sweep, start with the paddle in the same position as though you were going to paddle forwards, but this time the blade itself is on edge instead of flat. Put the blade in the water and sweep it in as wide an arc as you can right round to the stern of the canoe. If you have started on the right, this will turn the canoe to the left. (Fig. 47.)

To do the Stern Sweep, start with the paddle where you left it at the end of the Bow Sweep and take it in as wide an arc as possible to the bow. If you have started on the left, this will turn the canoe to the left. (Fig. 48.)

Therefore, if you do the Bow Sweep on your right and the Stern Sweep on your left, the canoe will revolve to the left. If you do the two strokes on the opposite sides (Bow left and Stern right) you revolve the other way.

Slap for Support on Recovery

The first of this pair, the Slap for Support, is designed to knock you upright should you unexpectedly begin to capsize. Unfortunately it is somewhat mis-named because you do not slap down on the water but rather pull yourself up on your paddle.

Notice, in Fig. 49, how the canoeist has his wrists underneath his paddle, how he is now pulling himself up with his right hand against the resistance the blade lying flat as it does on the water.

To practise this have the paddle horizontal with one blade flat and your hands as shown. Fall towards the flat blade and, when it hits the water pull yourself up. When you are upright, drop your hand to twist the blade through 90° and so take it out of the water again.

Please remember that you must practise this and all the other strokes equally well on both sides—in canoeing you have to be ambidextrous; the water does not know its left from its right and so you must be ready on either side.

Fig. 49

Draw Stroke

Now that you have done the Recovery Stroke, and we hope noticed exactly what the paddle blade does, please put the whole paddle as vertically as you can, out a little way from the side of the canoe and with the face (hollow side) of the blade flat towards the canoe, in the water. Draw it carefully towards you and in fact the canoe will move sideways towards the blade (Fig. 50). This is the Draw Stoke.

Just before the blade reaches the side of the canoe twist it quickly through 90° by dropping your hand, and push it gently out to where you started. Here again twist it through 90° so that it now is in the position at which you started.

Carry on pulling it in and pushing it out until you have got to where you want.

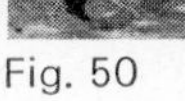

Fig. 50

Sculling for Support

The action of Sculling is the movement of the paddle so that the blade works on the water in a similar way to the blade of a propeller. In this pair of strokes we use this action firstly to hold us up and secondly to move us sideways again. Whereas in the previous strokes, Recovery and Draw, the action of each stroke was a once and for all, these two are continuous.

To Scull for Support (Fig. 51) the blade is laid flat on the water and then slightly tilted so that the leading edge of the blade (front edge if you are moving it forward, back edge as you move it backwards) is tilted upwards a little. Then you move it to and fro in a small arc on the water beside you, so that it skids over the water's surface.

When you have the action right you can begin to lean on your paddle and so rely upon the sculling action to keep you from capsizing.

The Sculling Draw

Now take your whole paddle, and, instead of having it horizontal in front of you, have it vertical beside you, with one blade in the water. As you move it a short distance to and fro in the water turn the leading edge slightly outwards (front edge forwards, back edge backwards) and your canoe will move sideways towards the side on which the paddle is (Fig. 52).

Beyond paddling forwards, these two basic sculling strokes are probably the most used of any as you progress. Therefore you should practise them until you have them working well. Do them **slowly** to start with, only getting fast after you are sure they are working correctly.

Figs. 51 and 52

ADVANCED PADDLING SKILLS

You must learn your Basic Skills so well that you no longer have to think about them when you do them. Then you will find that you can combine them; you can use the bit you want to use, to make the canoe go where you want. Pictures of three Advanced Skills are shown on this page. Can you see how they are made up?

Fig. 53

Fig. 54

Fig. 55

The Telemark

(Fig. 53) allows your canoe to be turned around in the eddies of the rapids. It is made up of Sculling for Support (with the back of the blade on the water) and the Stern Sweep.

The High Telemark

The High Telemark (Fig. 54) is much the same as the Telemark, except that the paddle is turned over so that the face of the blade is now working on the water instead of skidding over it, and it is helping you to turn the canoe.

The Bow Rudder

The Bow Rudder (Fig. 55) is useful for river canoeing because it is far better to steer the bow of the canoe than the stern. It can be described as a sort of Draw Stroke done at the bow. Look carefully at the position of the hands and the paddle and see how you get on with it.

Fig. 56 Draw Stroke by Kayak in Slalom

Fig. 57 Draw Stroke by Canadian in Slalom

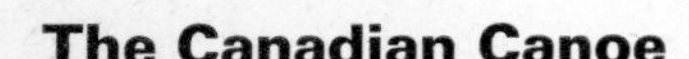

The Canadian Canoe

In our introduction we mentioned a similarity in the handling of the Canadian canoe and the Kayak canoe. We have now learnt enough about the handling of the latter to begin to see how to handle the former.

Look at Fig. 56 and you will soon see that we have talked about a stroke very like this, on page 30 in the Draw Stroke.

Now look at Fig. 57 and you will see that the Bow man in this C.2 Slalom Canadian is doing exactly the same thing as the man in the K.1 Slalom Kayak. The differences come, not in the action of the blade in the water which is precisely the same in both cases, but in the type of paddle in each case and the way it is being held.

Therefore, learning properly all that we have given you so far will help you to some extent in learning about Canadian canoes. But there is a lot more to learn as well, and when you have learnt it you will find the Canadian just as much fun as the Kayak.

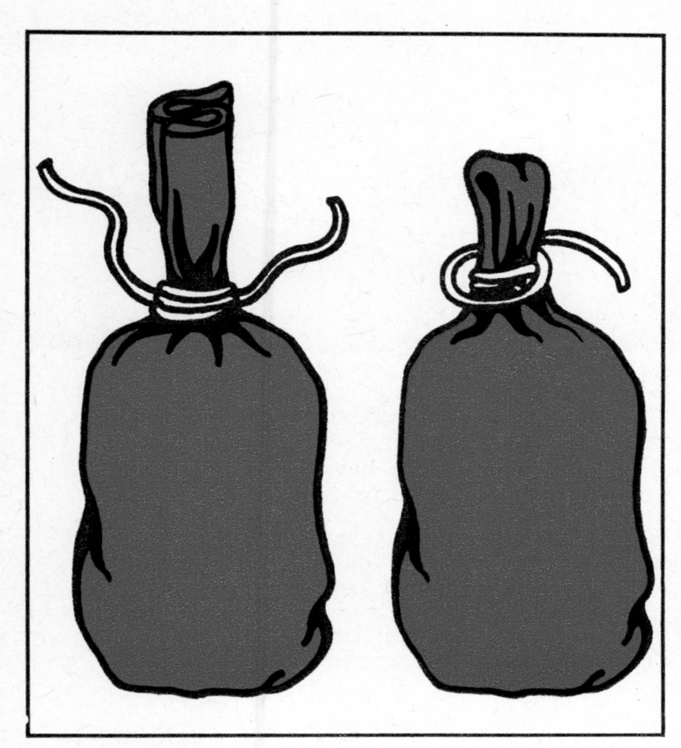

Fig. 58 Closing a waterproof kit bag

PACKING A CANOE

The job of packing your canoe for an extended journey has only a few simple rules and these are designed for your own safety and comfort. Here they are, in the order that they will come up as you pack.

Rule 1. Put everything that you should/ought/must keep dry in waterproof bags.

Rule 2. First In, Last Out. Put everything into your canoe in the reverse order to that which you will want to take them out.

Rule 3. Get everything out of **your** way.

Let us look at them one by one.

Rule 1. The things that you ought to keep dry are your bedding, your clothing, your matches and any perishable food you may have. According to the shape of the space available in your canoe, you can have many small or a few large packages. You can buy waterproof bags, or you can make them yourself out of light, rubberised canvas, Polythene bags are very easily snagged and torn. Therefore, if you are using these, use two, one inside the other, and do NOT use very light, thin polythene.

Fig. 58 shows you one way of closing the mouth of these bags. As this uses up quite a bit of the bag, it pays you to have long bags and not to pack them right up to the mouth.

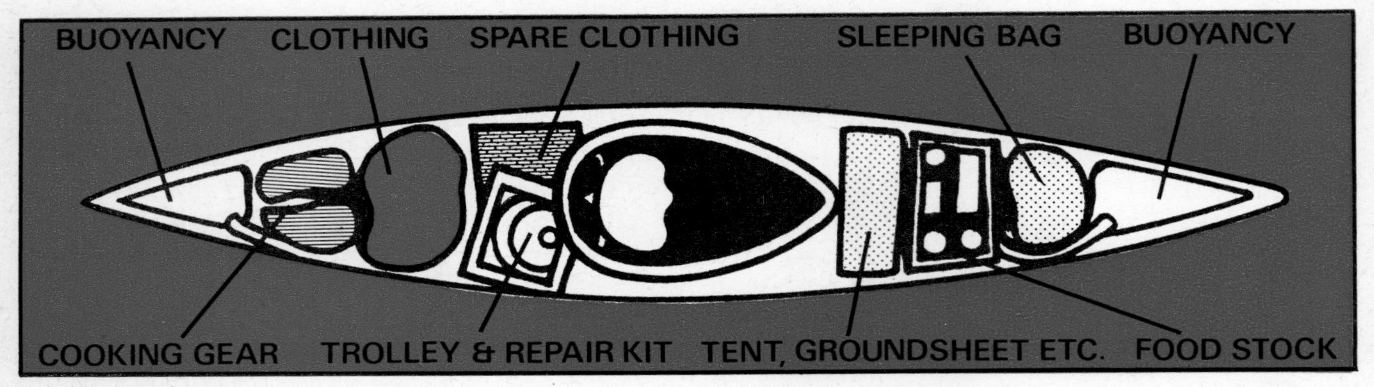

Fig. 59 A loaded canoe

Rule 2. F.I.L.O. As you will probably be making camp in a rainstorm, the last thing that you should pack into your canoe is your tent. As you want to go home in dry clothes, the first thing you put in is that bundle of clothes. Perhaps your bedding and your night-gear will come next because; since you have already got your tent up first at your arrival point, you can put these things straight inside.

You will find that other things come in their own order in due course, and you develop your own packing order. If you use a paraffin stove, pack it in its own, very old waterproof bag, not to keep the water out as they work perfectly well after getting wet, but to keep the paraffin in. Tins and things, if they have paper labels, should be marked with a waterproof felt pen on the lid as to what is inside; otherwise you will find yourself opening quite the wrong things for supper when the labels have been washed off.

Rule 3. Get everything out of **your** way. This is important. Your part of the canoe belongs to you and you alone. If you allow packages to be in your space with you, they will get in your way as you get in, and again when you get out. And you may have to get out in a hurry. **So no parcels in your part, please.**

Have a look at Fig. 59. It may be a bit neater than you can arrange, but at least things are in their right places.

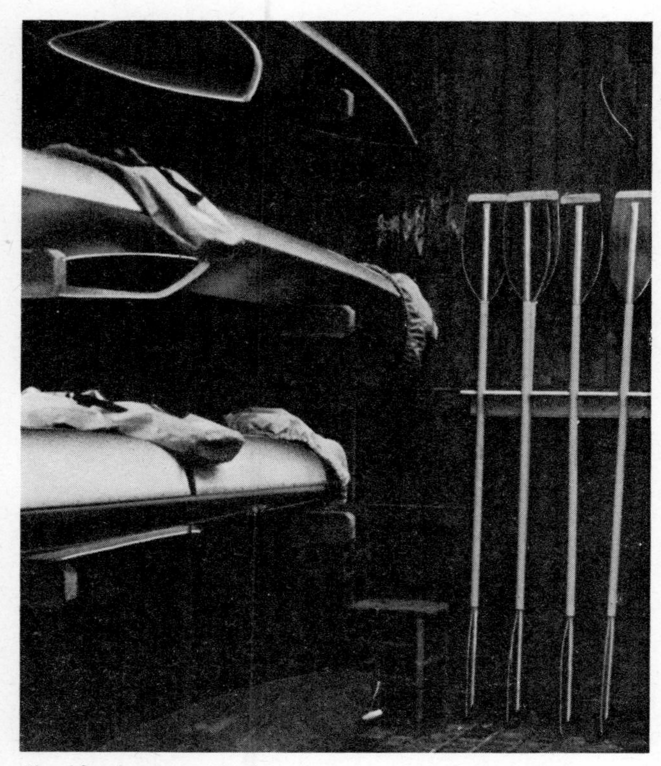

Fig. 60 Canoes on racks

STORING THE CANOE

It does not really matter how canoes are made, they should not be left outside in the damp of long grass. Even glass canoes will rot away in time if this is done to them, and the canvas-skinned canoes will rot away in a winter.

All canoes and equipment should be brought under cover, preferably into a dry, airy place. If you have a number they can be put on racks as in Fig. 60. If you have one and want it out of the way, you can sling it up into the roof of your garage or shed.

Everything should be washed and cleaned thoroughly before it is put away, and all repairs properly made at the same time. If there are wooden parts, or you have a wooden frame or skin to your canoe, you may need to rub it down and re-varnish it. Canvas may need re-dressing. Everything should be left in perfect order so that you can quickly get it all out and onto the water again as the first ray of warm sunshine comes through in the spring.

If you have a folding canoe, take it to bits and leave the skin spread out so that the air can get round that as well. At the same time you can inspect the framework, repair and re-varnish it as necessary before putting it away in its bags ready for a quick getaway next time.

In this way your canoe will last you a long, long time, and always be ready to take you afloat.

Fig. 61

SPRINT RACING

There are a lot of different ways in which you can go in for competition in a canoe. One of the oldest is that of Sprint Racing and we have a very old challenge trophy to compete for, called the Paddling Challenge Cup, which belongs to the Royal Canoe Club and was first raced for in 1874.

There are World Championships in Sprint Racing, and it is an Olympic sport as well, having been introduced by the Germans at Berlin in 1936.

We paddle in K.1s, K.2s, (men and women) and K.4s, (men only) over distances of 500 m, 1000 m, and 10,000 m. In England there has recently been built an International Sprint Racing Course at Holme Pierrepont just outside Nottingham, and our National Championships are held there.

Recently there has been introduced a special racing canoe for young people, called the Espada Youth K.1. This can be raced in their own championships by people of both sexes from 12 years old to 18. It is a G.R.P. canoe which you can make yourself and it is gaining in popularity very rapidly. It is well worth a try if you think Sprint Racing is your way to canoe.

Fig. 62

LONG DISTANCE RACING

If Sprint Racing is the track event in canoes, then Long Distance racing is the cross country version of the sport. Here you paddle in various classes of canoe—men and women—over distances of between 5–25 miles. You may paddle over the sea, or inland, or at times you may run out of water altogether, have to pick up your canoe and run with it to the next bit of water.

Long distance racing is not as old a form of competition as all that. It was started by a bet in a pub some years ago; but it did not really catch on until it developed from a bet as to how fast canoeists could travel between two points miles apart and became a genuine race. There is one exceptionally gruelling and long race in England, from Devizes to Westminster, run every Easter. It is not really a race but a competition, since competitors can start when they like and are timed over the 126 miles. Seniors do this distance and its 76 portages without stopping in a time knocking about 20 hours. Juniors have a compulsory stop overnight.

There are international L.D. races but there are as yet no World Championships. The classes of canoe include the Espada Youth K.1 so, if you have one of these, you can compete in this as well as Sprint.

SLALOM

Slalom is another competition, but this time you are going to compete individually on a very rough rapid over which green and white, and red and white poles have been hung in pairs called 'gates'. You have to manoeuvre your canoe through these gates so that you pass the red one on your port or lefthand side and the green one on your starboard or righthand side. There is a fairly complicated system of penalties for when you hit the poles or miss the gates, and these are added to your time to make the final result. Obviously the competitor who completes the course in the least time, having the least penalties is the winner, so the lowest score wins.

This competition was started somewhere in the Alps in the 1930s, and goes extremely well with ski-ing. In fact some of the terms used are common to both sports. The first World Championships event was held in Geneva in 1949 and the West Germans brought it into the Olympic Games in 1972, with the first ever artificial slalom course at Augsburg. It is very popular in Britain and we have won a gold medal and a number of silver and bronze ones as well.

Fig. 63

Fig. 64

WILD WATER RACING

Wild (or White) Water Racing is in fact also a competition. For many years people had toured down rapid rivers and enjoyed themselves. Occasionally, we suspect, they had raced each other in places. In 1969 the French offered a World Championship on the river Vezere but, because it would have been impossible to have everybody start together in such a small river, they decided to start people off at minute intervals and time them. It has remained thus ever since.

In this island there is not really enough water in our rivers, nor are our rapids heavy enough or long enough to sustain a really good course (usually about 6–10 km on the Continent). Nevertheless some good events are run, and in one or two cases the local authority that controls the river lets out an amount of water from a reservoir and so causes a minor flood and better rapids down the river.

Nevertheless we do quite well in International events. A special type of racing Kayak has been developed for the sport. It is very exhilarating and well worth going in for.

CANOE ORIENTEERING

Only a little orienteering has been done in canoes as yet. However, it is a sport which has excellent potential in areas where the water is much broken up by islands. Old wet gravel workings are eminently suitable for it, and some first class matches have been held in that wonderful lake of a myriad islands in Ireland, the Upper Lough Erne.

In canoe orienteering an adaptation of point to point orienteering will probably be best on most rivers, whereas on lakes and estuaries score orienteering may be better. Only rarely, as on Upper Lough Erne, will the consecutive point to point type of orienteering be possible.

Canoe orienteers, whether in single or double canoes, must have mastery over their canoes, for calm lakes and certainly lochs, can soon become violent. In all forms of orienteering competition the essence of the sport is that those taking part should break fresh ground. Therefore, the ability to carry out good self-rescue operations such as deep water rescues or even the Eskimo Roll becomes absolutely essential.

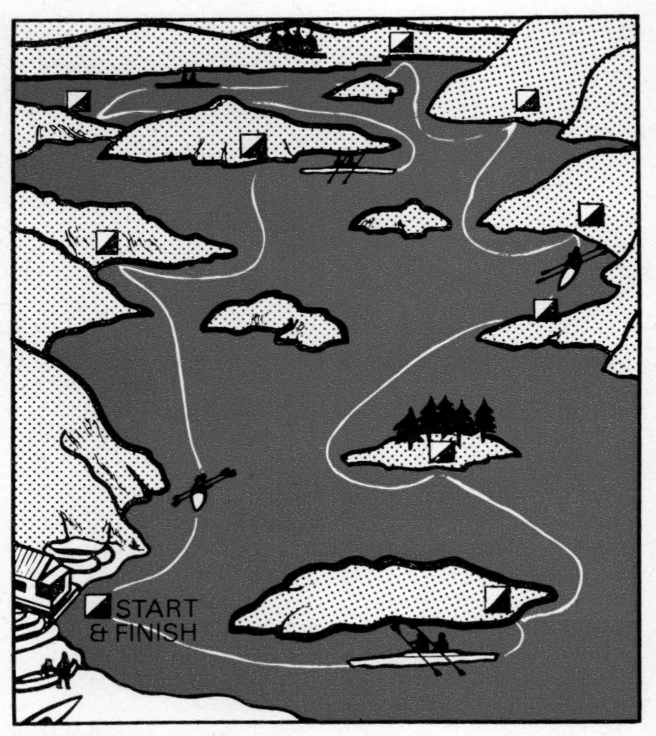

Fig. 65

Fig. 66

CANOE POLO

Here is a very new form of competition in the canoeing world. Canoe Polo has been played for a good many years as a 'fun' game, using a football and perhaps opposite banks of a river as the goals.

Then it was played in BAT canoes as a five-a-side match at the National Canoe Exhibition in 1969 and immediately it was seized upon as a first class game. Rules were made, and it has now become a serious five-a-side competition to National Championships every year at the National Canoe Exhibition in February. The area of play is approximately the same as that of water polo, but the goals are boards 1 m square hung above the centre at each end so that the lower edge is 2 m above the water. Play is about 7 minutes each way, and great skill is appearing among players, both in handling the ball and in dealing with their opponents.

Competitions are played all over the country, and there is no doubt that Canoe Polo is going to be a vigorous section of our competition world.

SURFING

Here is another very new form of competition. People have been surfing in canoes for quite a long time, but the idea of making it a competition was not born until the Beach Master at Bude, an ex-Royal Naval deep sea diver, suggested it. A lesson from an Australian Surf Life Saving veteran on how to judge Malibu board riding gave us the clue to judging canoes in surf also. The surf canoeist is an acrobat, looping the loop, twisting and rolling, and using each wave to the best advantage in getting his Kayak to manoeuvre in this way. His is the gift of understanding the surf, of 'reading' the waves so that he knows how they will carry him and allow him to perform. It is glorious and exhilarating, both to watch and even better to do yourself.

Besides just that, there are straight sprint races, out through the surf, round a mark and back to the beach again. There are relays and many other events to create one of the most wonderful competitions of all. But don't start in the big stuff at Bude. Tackle first lesser surf on the many beaches all the way round our island. Look at the map on Page 46. There is sure to be some beach within your reach where you can start. Don't be surprised at the amount of swimming ashore you have to do to start with. It is all part of the game and quite safe so long as you are careful.

Fig. 67

Fig. 68

CANOE LIFE GUARDS

And so lastly to the Corps of Canoe Life Guards, to that part of canoeing where you can go to the help of other people who are in difficulties, who are in distress on or in the water for one reason or another.

It is difficult for people outside the sport to appreciate the immense value of this frail little craft in helping other people. Its very versatility is the reason for this. It will go where no other vessel can go. It will face rough water which would destroy other craft. Yet even in these waters it remains so easy to handle that the canoeist can render assistance to others.

To try to enumerate the types of rescues that have been carried out by members of the Corps is impossible in this little book. Many of them have appeared to the canoeist to be so easy that he may have failed to report it, reckoning it all in the day's work. Much of the work of the members is straight forward anyway, like accompanying long distance swimmers in their ocean swimming, or escorting parties of less experienced canoeists on their ordinary journeys. But to join with a lifeboat crew in the salvaging of a vessel stuck on a sandbank is a job which needs skill, and stamina, and the ability to stick at it even though the conditions are hard and rough, and have no glamour at all while you are at it.

This is the most exciting, exhilarating and rewarding canoeing of all.

WHERE TO CANOE

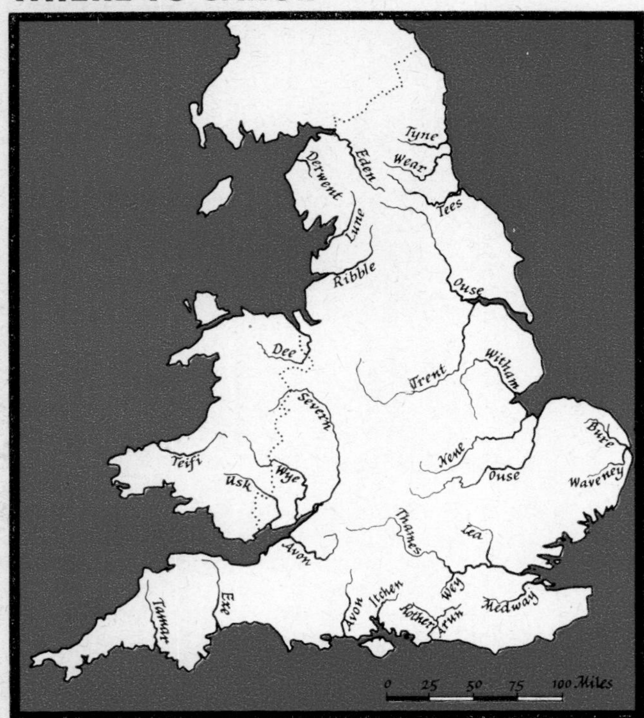

Fig. 69

WHERE TO SURF

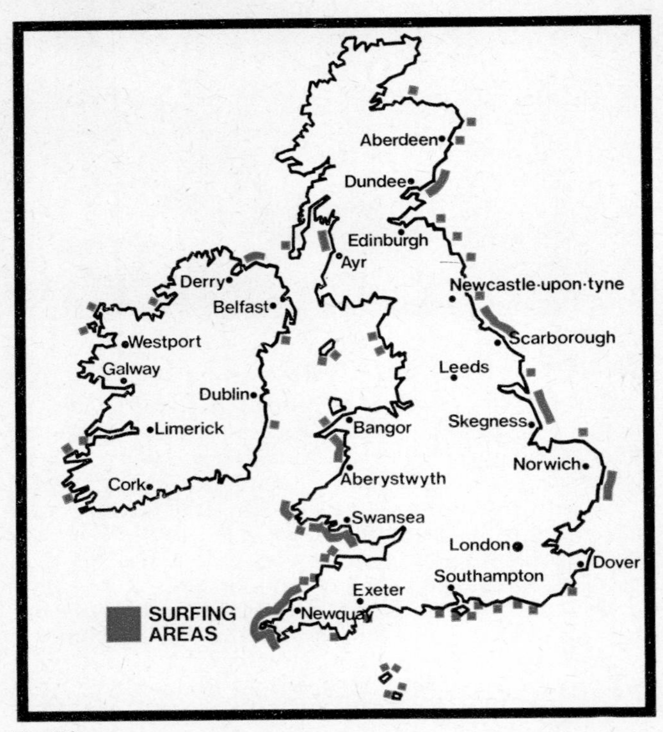

Fig. 70